"A time is coming and has now come when the true worshipers will worship the Father in spirit and truth, for they are the kind of worshipers the Father seeks."

Vineyard Music Group is dedicated to the vision of seeing our nation bow before the Lord in worship. It is our hope that these praise & worship songs bring you into the almighty presence of God in a powerful and anointed manner. Each series introduces an exciting new facet of worship allowing the listener to experience worship of the Father in spirit and in truth. VINEYARD MUSIC GROUP is a full-service worship and praise music company. We hope that this songbook is a valuable resource in facilitating worship whenever you use it.

PRAISE & WORSHIP CDs AND TAPES
Experience the music known world-wide for its power and intimacy. From dynamic live worship albums to high-quality devotional and inspirational recordings, encounter the glory of God through the beauty of music.

SONGBOOKS
Specially designed for your worship needs, the worship and praise songbooks Volumes 1 - 5 are arranged for lyrics, guitar and piano; and a Words Only Songbook is available.

Worship Product Lines Available through Vineyard Music Group:

TOUCHING THE FATHER'S HEART
Enjoy the fluid, spontaneous dynamics of a live praise and worship service. This series provides one of today's most unique approaches to involving listeners in a live worship experience.

WORSHIP SONGS OF THE VINEYARD
Each album features renown soloists, duos and group vocalists as they interpret the beauty and simplicity of Vineyard songs with a refined studio sound.

BEST LOVED WORSHIP & PRAISE SONGS FROM THE VINEYARD
Featuring praise and worship favorites, this series contains collections of songs worshipers know and love.

continued...

VINEYARD PSALMS
These collections contain only the most intimate Vineyard worship songs that allow the listener to enter into a spirit of worship during their quiet time.

CLASSICAL AND INSTRUMENTAL SERIES
Reflective and intimate songs presented through professional arrangements featuring some of Vineyard's most popular songs. The Classical Series (Volumes I and II) utilize the beauty of classical guitar while the Instrumental Series (four titles) presents calming worship songs with full orchestration.

VINEYARD WORSHIP FOR KIDS SERIES
The Worship for Kids series are contemporary recordings produced for young kids who desire to grow in worship. This series offers professional musicianship with the dynamic of children singing.

For more information, or for questions and comments regarding Vineyard music, please contact:

Vineyard Music Group
P.O. Box 68025 • Anaheim, CA 92817-0825
or call **1-800-852-VINE**
or FAX (714) 777-8119

All songs in this songbook are subject to the full copyright notice for each song as listed in this publication. All rights are reserved. The words of the songs in this book may only be reproduced by obtaining permission from the copyright owner of the individual song. Users of this songbook are reminded that reproduction of any song published here by any means, without express permission of the copyright owner, is a violation of the law.

©1994 Mercy/Vineyard Publishing
Administered by Music Services
209 Chappelwood Dr., Franklin, TN 37064
(615) 794-9015
FAX (615) 794-0793

CONTENTS

ALL SEASONS 4	LORD, GLORIFY YOUR NAME 98
ALLELUIA 6	LORD MY GOD 100
BEAUTIFUL TO ME 8	LORD OF ALL 102
BLESSED ARE THEY 10	LORD OF CREATION 104
BLESSED BE THE NAME OF THE LORD 12	LORD WE PRAISE YOU 106
CALL THE ELDERS 14	LOVE OF MY LIFE 108
CHANGED BY YOUR GLORY 16	MESSIAH 110
CLOSER TO THEE 18	MY DESIRE 112
COME FILL THIS PLACE 20	MY HEART CRIES HOLY 114
COME FILL US AGAIN 22	MY REDEEMER 116
CONSUME ME WITH YOUR LOVE 24	NO ONE BUT YOU 118
COVER ME 26	NOTHING CAN COMPARE 120
✓ CROWN HIM WITH MANY CROWNS 28	ONE THING I ASK 122
DELIVERER 30	ONLY BY YOUR PRESENCE 124
EVERY BREATH THAT I TAKE 32	PRECIOUS CHILD 126
✓ FAITHFUL ONE 34	PRECIOUS CORNERSTONE 128
FATHER 36	PSALM 121 (I LIFT MY EYES UP) 130
FATHER, I WANT YOU TO HOLD ME 38	PSALM 23 132
FOREVER 40	REDEEMED 134
GIVE HIM PRAISE 42	REDEEMER 136
GIVE ME LIFE HOLY SPIRIT 44	REFINER'S FIRE 138
GLORIOUS 46	REJOICE 140
GLORY IN THE HIGHEST 48	SHINE JESUS SHINE 142
GLORY TO THE LORD 50	SHOUT FOR JOY 144
GOD IS SO GOOD 52	SING PRAISES 146
HE HAS OVERCOME 54	SOFTEN MY HEART 148
HEARTS ON FIRE 56	THE LORD REIGNS 150
HOLINESS UNTO THE LORD 58	THE VICTORY IS THE LORD'S 152
I BELIEVE YOU LORD 60	THIS DAY 154
I GIVE MY LIFE 62	TO BE WITH YOU 156
I GIVE YOU PRAISE 64	UNENDING LOVE 158
I RECEIVE YOU 66	UNTO THE KING 160
I SING A NEW SONG 68	WALKIN' IN THE KINGDOM 162
I WILL CHANGE YOUR NAME 70	WARRIOR 164
I WILL SING OF THE MERCIES 72	WE ARE YOUR CHURCH 166
I'M YOURS 74	WE CRY HOLY 168
ISAIAH 40 76	WE REJOICE IN YOU 170
✓ ISN'T HE 78	WHEN I BOW DOWN 172
I'VE GOT MY ARMOR ON 80	WORDS CAN NEVER SAY 174
JESUS WE LOVE AND PRAISE YOU 82	WORTHY IS THE LAMB 176
KING OF SAINTS 84	YOU ARE MIGHTY 178
LEAD ME 88	YOU ARE THE KING WHO REIGNS 180
LET FORGIVENESS FLOW 90	YOU ARE THE REASON 182
LET THE REDEEMED 92	YOU OH LORD ARE A GREAT GOD 184
LET US GO INTO THE HOUSE OF THE LORD 94	YOU WILL REIGN 186
LIGHT OF THE WORLD 96	YOUR WAYS ARE MARVELOUS 188

ALL SEASONS

Words and Music by
DANNY DANIELS

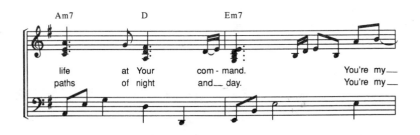

© 1988 Mercy Publishing
All Rights Reserved. International Copyright Secured.
Use With Permission Only.

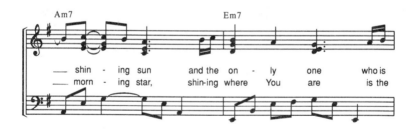
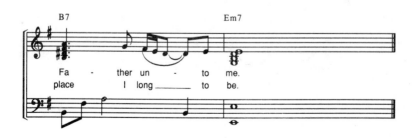

ALLELUIA

Words and Music by
CARL TUTTLE

© 1982 Mercy Publishing
All Rights Reserved. International Copyright Secured
Use With Permission Only.

BEAUTIFUL TO ME

Words and Music by
ANDY PARK

© 1989 Mercy Publishing
All Rights Reserved. International Copyright Secured.
Use With Permission Only.

BLESSED BE THE NAME OF THE LORD

Words and Music by
KEVIN PROSCH AND DANNY DANIELS

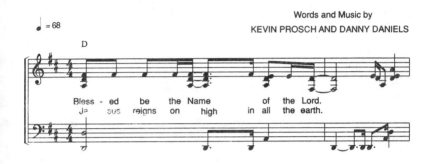

© 1989 Mercy Publishing
All Rights Reserved. International Copyright Secured.
Use With Permission Only.

CHANGED BY YOUR GLORY

Words and Music by
ANDY PARK

© 1989 Mercy Publishing
All Rights Reserved. International Copyright Secured.
Use With Permission Only.

CLOSER TO THEE

Words and Music by
EDDIE ESPINOSA

Lord I want to be clos-er and clos-er to

Thee, take my heart and lead me
guide my steps and lead me
I can feel You draw-ing me
I can hear You call-ing me

Fine

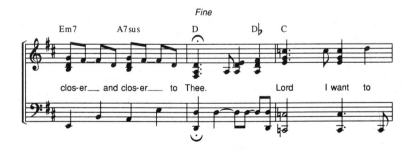

clos-er and clos-er to Thee. Lord I want to

© 1982 Mercy Publishing
All Rights Reserved. International Copyright Secured.
Use With Permission Only.

COME FILL THIS PLACE

Words and Music by
CINDY GOUGH

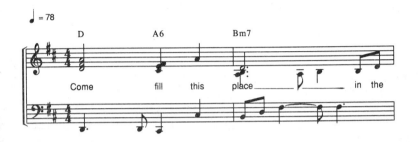

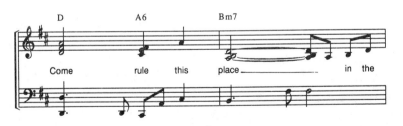

© 1988 Mercy Publishing
All Rights Reserved. International Copyright Secured.
Use With Permission Only.

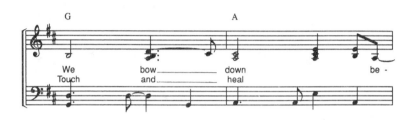
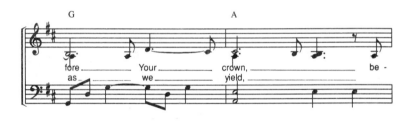

CONSUME ME WITH YOUR LOVE

Words and Music by
EDDIE ESPINOSA & CINDY RETHMEIER

© 1989 Mercy Publishing
All Rights Reserved. International Copyright Secured.
Use With Permission Only.

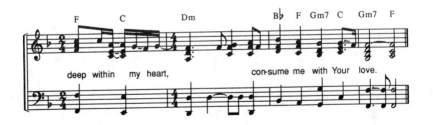

COVER ME

Words and Music by
DANNY DANIELS

CROWN HIM WITH MANY CROWNS

DELIVERER

Words and Music by
RANDY & TERRY BUTLER

© 1988 Mercy Publishing
All Rights Reserved. International Copyright Secured.
Use With Permission Only.

EVERY BREATH THAT I TAKE

FAITHFUL ONE

Words and Music by
BRIAN DOERKSEN

© 1989 Mercy Publishing
All Rights Reserved. International Copyright Secured.
Use With Permission Only.

FATHER

Words and Music by
DANNY DANIELS

© 1989 Mercy Publishing
All Rights Reserved. International Copyright Secured.
Use With Permission Only.

FOREVER

Words and Music by
DANNY DANIELS

© 1989 Mercy Publishing
All Rights Reserved. International Copyright Secured.
Use With Permission Only.

GIVE HIM PRAISE

GIVE ME LIFE HOLY SPIRIT

GLORIOUS

Words and Music by
HOLLAND DAVIS & JOHN LAI

© 1987 Mercy Publishing
All Rights Reserved. International Copyright Secured.
Use With Permission Only.

GLORY IN THE HIGHEST

Words and Music by
JOHN BARNETT

O be-hold how good He is, _____
Je-sus how we love You, _____

our Lord God Most High. _____

Bless-ings fall-ing from His throne, _____
And to feel Your Spir - it _____

© 1988 Mercy Publishing
All Rights Reserved. International Copyright Secured.
Use With Permission Only.

GLORY TO THE LORD

Words and Music by
SCOTT BRENNER

© 1987 Mercy Publishing
All Rights Reserved. International Copyright Secured.
Use With Permission Only.

GOD IS SO GOOD

Words and Music by
KEVIN PROSCH

(And) God _____ is so good. _____ (And)

God _____ is so good. _____ 1. 2. He rides __ up- on __
3. You reign __ on high __

the wings __ of the wind, He is __ ex - alt -
in maj - es - ty, (and) the wid - ow's heart __

ed by His __ name Jah. __ He walks __ in the midst
caus - es __ to sing. __ You hear __ the cry

© 1990 Mercy Publishing
All Rights Reserved. International Copyright Secured.
Use With Permission Only.

HE HAS OVERCOME

Words and Music by
CAROL HERNANDEZ & STEVE SJOGREN

© 1988 Mercy Publishing
All Rights Reserved. International Copyright Secured.
Use With Permission Only.

HEARTS ON FIRE

Words and Music by
DANNY DANIELS

© 1989 Mercy Publishing
All Rights Reserved. International Copyright Secured.
Use With Permission Only.

I BELIEVE YOU LORD

Words and Music by
CARL TUTTLE

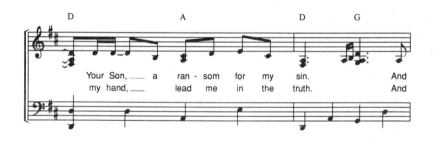

© 1987 Mercy Publishing
All Rights Reserved. International Copyright Secured
Use With Permission Only.

I GIVE MY LIFE

Words and Music by
MARC NELSON

© 1988 Mercy Publishing
All Rights Reserved. International Copyright Secured.
Use With Permission Only.

I GIVE YOU PRAISE

Words and Music by
DANNY DANIELS

© 1988 Mercy Publishing
All Rights Reserved. International Copyright Secured.
Use With Permission Only.

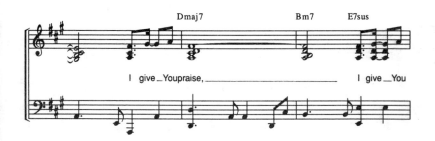

I RECEIVE YOU

Words and Music by
JOHN LAI

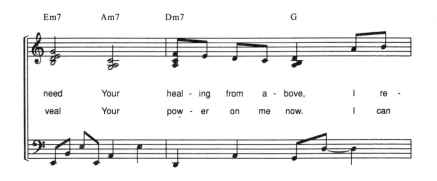

© 1982 Mercy Publishing
All Rights Reserved. International Copyright Secured.
Use With Permission Only.

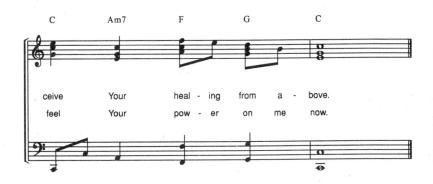

I SING A NEW SONG

Words and Music by
CARL TUTTLE & JOHN WIMBER

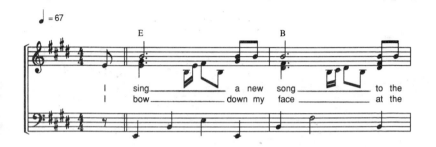

© 1982 Mercy Publishing
All Rights Reserved. International Copyright Secured.
Use With Permission Only.

I WILL CHANGE YOUR NAME

Words and Music by
D. J. BUTLER

© 1987 Mercy Publishing
All Rights Reserved. International Copyright Secured.
Use With Permission Only.

I WILL SING OF THE MERCIES

Words and Music by
JOHN BARNETT

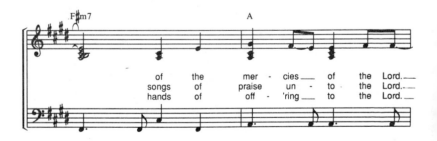

© 1988 Mercy Publishing
All Rights Reserved. International Copyright Secured.
Use With Permission Only.

I'M YOURS

Words and Music by
EDDIE ESPINOSA

© 1982 Mercy Publishing
All Rights Reserved. International Copyright Secured.
Use With Permission Only.

ISAIAH 40

Words and Music by
ANDY PARK

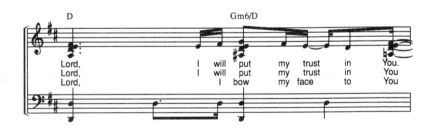

© 1989 Mercy Publishing
All Rights Reserved. International Copyright Secured.
Use With Permission Only.

ISN'T HE

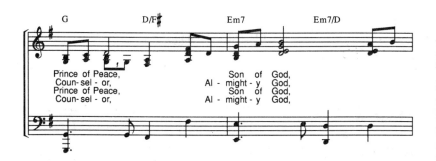
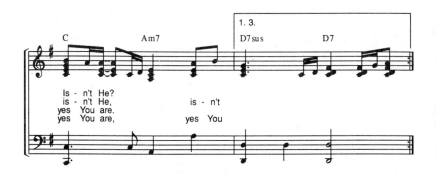

I'VE GOT MY ARMOR ON

JESUS WE LOVE AND PRAISE YOU

Words and Music by
MARC NELSON

© 1988 Mercy Publishing
All Rights Reserved. International Copyright Secured.
Use With Permission Only.

KING OF SAINTS

Words and Music by
KEVIN PROSCH

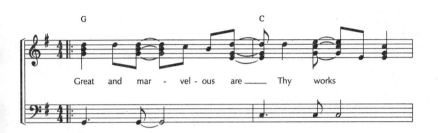
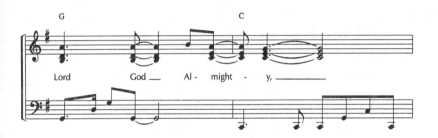

© 1987 Mercy Publishing
All Rights Reserved. International Copyright Secured.
Use With Permission Only.

Verse 2:
Lord I need You to guide me.
The path I walk is not my own
I am not able to make my way if left alone.

I need You beside me
To speak Your truth into my life
To know I can make it, even in the darkest night.

LET FORGIVENESS FLOW

Words and Music by
DANNY DANIELS

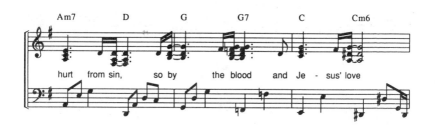

© 1989 Mercy Publishing
All Rights Reserved. International Copyright Secured.
Use With Permission Only.

LET US GO INTO THE HOUSE OF THE LORD

Words and Music by
REBECCA WILMARTH

© 1974 Rebecca Wilmarth/Admin. by Mercy Publishing
All Rights Reserved. International Copyright Secured.
Use With Permission Only.

LIGHT OF THE WORLD

Words and Music by
DANNY DANIELS

© 1987 Mercy Publishing
All Rights Reserved. International Copyright Secured.
Use With Permission Only.

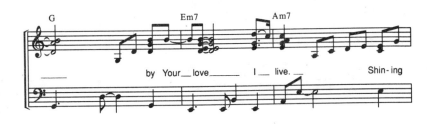

LORD, GLORIFY YOUR NAME

Words and Music by
ROBERT HARTMAN

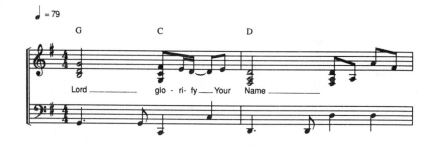

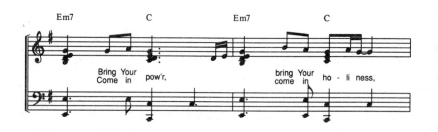

© 1989 Mercy Publishing
All Rights Reserved. International Copyright Secured.
Use With Permission Only.

LORD OF ALL

Words and Music by
DANNY DANIELS

© 1989 Mercy Publishing
All Rights Reserved. International Copyright Secured.
Use With Permission Only.

LORD WE PRAISE YOU

Words and Music by
DANNY DANIELS

© 1989 Mercy Publishing
All Rights Reserved. International Copyright Secured.
Use With Permission Only.

LOVE OF MY LIFE

Words and Music by
GINA PRAINO

© 1988 Mercy Publishing
All Rights Reserved. International Copyright Secured.
Use With Permission Only.

MESSIAH

Words and Music by
ANDY PARK

MY DESIRE

Words and Music by
CRAIG MUSSEAU

My de-sire is to wor - ship on - ly

You, You a - lone.

© 1989 Mercy Publishing
All Rights Reserved. International Copyright Secured.
Use With Permission Only.

MY HEART CRIES HOLY

MY REDEEMER

Words and Music by
SUSAN COSTANTINI

© 1988 Mercy Publishing
All Rights Reserved. International Copyright Secured.
Use With Permission Only

NO ONE BUT YOU

Words and Music by
JOHN WIMBER

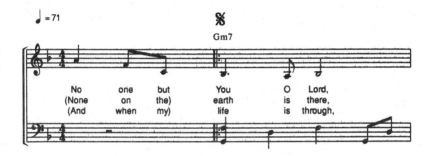

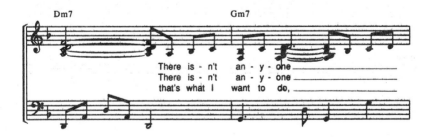

© 1982 Mercy Publishing
All Rights Reserved. International Copyright Secured.
Use With Permission Only.

123

ONLY BY YOUR PRESENCE

PRECIOUS CORNERSTONE

Words and Music by
ANDY PARK

© 1989 Mercy Publishing
All Rights Reserved. International Copyright Secured.
Use With Permission Only.

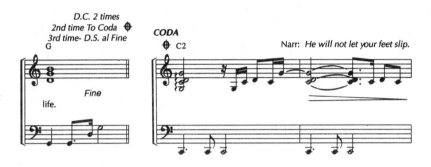

He who watches over you will not slumber. Indeed, He who watches over Israel will neither slumber nor sleep. The Lord watches over you. The Lord is the shade of your right

hand. The sun will not harm you by day, nor the moon by night. The Lord will keep you from all harm. He will watch over your life. The Lord will warch over your coming and going.

Both now and forever more. Oh how I need You Lord.

PSALM 23

REDEEMER

Words and Music by
CINDY RETHMEIER

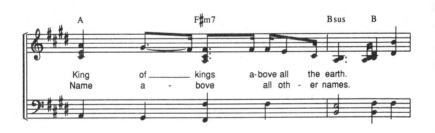

© 1989 Mercy Publishing
All Rights Reserved. International Copyright Secured.
Use With Permission Only.

REJOICE

Words and Music by
PATRICK SWAGERTY

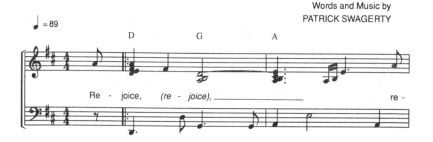
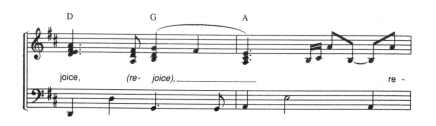
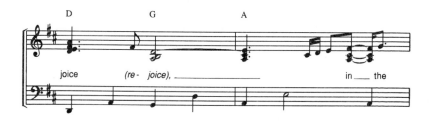

© 1988 Mercy Publishing
All Rights Reserved. International Copyright Secured.
Use With Permission Only.

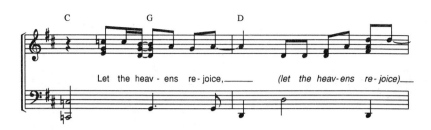
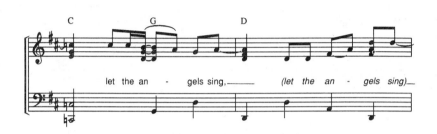

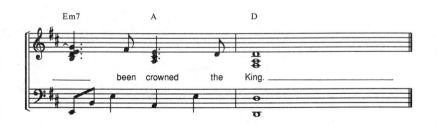

SHINE JESUS SHINE

2. Lord, I come to your awesome presence
From the shadows into your radiance
By the blood I may enter your brightness
Search me, try me, consume all my darkness
Shine on me, shine on me

3. As we gaze on your kingly brightness
So our faces display your likeness
Ever changing from glory to glory
Mirrored here may our lives tell your story
Shine on me, shine on me

SHOUT FOR JOY

SING PRAISES

Words and Music by
JUDE DEL HIERRO

© 1987 Mercy Publishing
All Rights Reserved. International Copyright Secured.
Use With Permission Only.

SOFTEN MY HEART

Words and Music by
CINDY GOUGH

© 1989 Mercy Publishing
All Rights Reserved. International Copyright Secured.
Use With Permission Only.

THE LORD REIGNS

Words and Music by
RICK FOUNDS

2. In your presence Lord *(In your presence Lord)*
   The mountains melt like wax *(The mountains melt like wax)*
   (repeat)

   In your presence Lord *(In your presence Lord)*
   I bow before your throne *(I bow before your throne)*
   (repeat)

3. I lift my hands *(I lift my hands)*
   And worship You oh Lord *(And worship You oh Lord)*
   (repeat)

   For You are the Lord *(For You are the Lord)*
   Most high above the earth *(Most high above the earth)*
   (repeat)

THE VICTORY IS THE LORD'S

Words and Music by
KEVIN PROSCH

153

THIS DAY

Words and Music by
JERRY & TARESA CHUCULATE

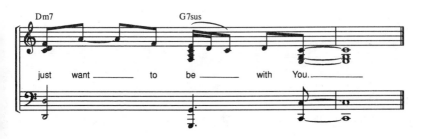

UNENDING LOVE

Words and Music by
JOHN BARNETT

© 1989 Mercy Publishing
All Rights Reserved. International Copyright Secured.
Use With Permission Only.

2. I receive your favor, your unending love
   Not because I've earned it, not for what I've done
   Just because You love me and I love your Son
   I know your favor, unending love

3. It's the presence of your kingdom as your glory fills this place
   And I see how much You love me as I look into your face
   Nothing could be better, there's nothing I would trade
   For your favor, unending love.

WALKIN' IN THE KINGDOM

Words and Music by
DANNY DANIELS

I am walk-in' in the king-dom of God, walk-in' in the
prais-in' prais-in'
danc-in' danc-in'

king-dom of God. Je-sus is my King,

I'm gon-na walk with Him. Now I'm walk-
praise His Name. Well I'm prais-
dance with Him. Well I'm danc-

© 1987 Mercy Publishing
All Rights Reserved. International Copyright Secured.
Use With Permission Only.

165

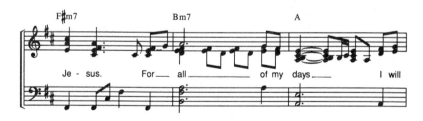

WE ARE YOUR CHURCH

Words and Music by
ANDY PARK

WE CRY HOLY

Words and Music by
ANDY PARK

© 1989 Mercy Publishing
All Rights Reserved. International Copyright Secured.
Use With Permission Only.

WE REJOICE IN YOU

**Words and Music by
DAVID BOYD**

♩ = 120

You are wor-thy, God my Lord, to be praised in song our hearts in one ac-cord. Let the sound of re-joic-ing fill your heart, we re-joice in You Je-sus, let us start to re-joice in

© 1988 Mercy Publishing
All Rights Reserved. International Copyright Secured.
Use With Permission Only.

WORDS CAN NEVER SAY

© 1985 Mercy Publishing
All Rights Reserved. International Copyright Secured.
Use With Permission Only.

YOU ARE MIGHTY

Words and Music by
CRAIG MUSSEAU

© 1989 Mercy Publishing
All Rights Reserved. International Copyright Secured.
Use With Permission Only.

YOU ARE THE KING WHO REIGNS

Words and Music by
DAVID BOYD

© 1982 Mercy Publishing
All Rights Reserved. International Copyright Secured.
Use With Permission Only.

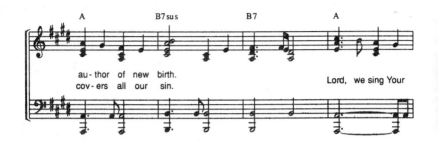

YOU ARE THE REASON

Words and Music by
PATTY KENNEDY

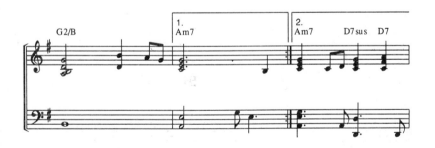

© 1987 Mercy Publishing
All Rights Reserved. International Copyright Secured.
Use With Permission Only.

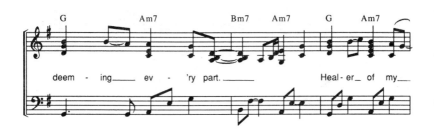

YOU OH LORD ARE A GREAT GOD

Words and Music by
TERRY & RANDY BUTLER

© 1989 Mercy Publishing
All Rights Reserved. International Copyright Secured.
Use With Permission Only.

YOUR WAYS ARE MARVELOUS

Words and Music by
ANDY PARK

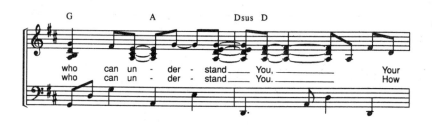

© 1989 Mercy Publishing
All Rights Reserved. International Copyright Secured.
Use With Permission Only.

WORSHIP PRODUCT AVAILABLE FROM VINEYARD MUSIC GROUP

WORSHIP SONGS OF THE VINEYARD
- 9101 1 - Hosanna
- 9100 2 - You Are Here
- 9103 3 - Come Holy Spirit
- 9104 4 - Glory
- 9105 5 - Draw Me Closer
- 9107 6 - We Welcome You
- 9110 7 - No One But You
- 9120 8 - Give Him Praise
- 9127 9 - I Want To Know You
- 9134 10 - Refiners Fire
- 9156 11 - Bring Your Kingdom
- 9164 12 - Lord Over All
- 9148 13 - Devoted To You
- 9150 14 - Send Your Spirit
- 9161 15 - Seek Righteousness
- 9167 16 - Great Is Your Mercy
- 9171 17 - Glory And Honor
- 9175 18 - Light The Fire Again
- 9181 19 - Everlasting Grace

TOUCHING THE FATHER'S HEART
- 9113 1 - Unto The King
- 9114 2 - Holy & Anointed One
- 9115 3 - We Exalt Your Name
- 9118 4 - Holiness Unto The Lord
- 9119 5 - King Of Saints
- 9122 6 - Fire Of God
- 9126 7 - Hear Our Cry
- 9128 8 - We Behold You
- 9131 9 - Take Our Lives
- 9135 10 - Save Us Oh God
- 9139 11 - I Bow Down
- 9144 12 - Throne Of Grace

COLLECTIONS
- 9109 Vineyard Collection Vol. I
- 9130 Vineyard Collection Vol II
- 9154 Vineyard Collection Vol. III
- 9155 Vineyard Psalms Vol. I
- 9166 Vineyard Psalms Vol. II
- 9176 Vineyard Psalms Vol. III
- 9172 The Best Loved Vol. I
- 9178 The Best Loved Vol. II

INSTRUMENTAL
- 9108 1 - Tender Mercy
- 9112 2 - Closer To Thee
- 9123 3 - Faithful One
- 9137 4 - Desire Only You
- 9138 Classical Vineyard I
- 9162 Classical Vineyard II

Continued...

All titles available in cassette and CD at your local Christian Bookstore

KIDS
- 9106 Worship For Kids 1 Cassette Only
- 9111 Worship For Kids 2 Cassette Only
- 9125 Worship For Kids 3 Cassette Only
- 9136 Worship For Kids 4 Cassette Only

SPECIALTY ALBUMS
- 9129 A Vineyard Christmas
- 9160 Vineyard Celebration
- 9173 Resurrection Celebration
- 9174 Con Mis Labios - Spanish Worship
- 9182 Contemporary Hymns & Classic Choruses
- 9185 A Christmas Celebration

SONGBOOKS
- FLB9100 Songs Of The Vineyard Volume 1
- FLB9121 Songs Of The Vineyard Volume 2
- FLB9145 Songs Of The Vineyard Volume 3
- FLB9165 Songs Of The Vineyard Volume 4
- VNB9170 Songs Of The Vineyard Volume 5